To Rev. Gloria Solomon,

Thank you for your
friendship and mentorship
for all these many
years.

David

WISDOM,
WARNINGS,
AND
WAKE-UP
CALLS

Annie Ruth's
TRUTHS

*Collected
and written
by*

**DAVID
PRESTON
SHARP**

WOOD LAKE

DEDICATION

Thanks, Mom ... I mean, Annie Ruth

Editor: Mike Schwartzentruber
Proofreader: Dianne Greenslade
Designer: Robert MacDonald

Library and Archives Canada Cataloguing in Publication
Title: Annie Ruth's truths : wisdom, warnings, and wake-up calls /
collected and written by David Preston Sharp.
Names: Ruth, Annie, 1934- author. | Sharp, David (David Preston), author, editor.
Identifiers: Canadiana (print) 2020034417X | Canadiana (ebook) 2020034451X |
ISBN 9781773432830 (softcover) | ISBN 9781773432847 (HTML) |
Subjects: LCSH: Ruth, Annie, 1934- – Quotations. | LCSH: African American women – Southern
States – Quotations. | LCSH: African Americans – Southern States – Quotations. | LCGFT: Sayings.
Classification: LCC PN6081.3 R87 2020 | DDC 081.089/96073–dc23

ISBN 978-1-77343-283-0

Published by Wood Lake Publishing Inc.
485 Beaver Lake Road, Kelowna, BC, Canada, V4V 1S5
www.woodlake.com | 250.766.2778

Wood Lake Publishing acknowledges the financial support of the Government of Canada.
Wood Lake Publishing acknowledges the financial support of the Province of British Columbia
through the Book Publishing Tax Credit.

Wood Lake Publishing acknowledges that we operate in the unceded territory
of the Syilx/Okanagan People, and we work to support reconciliation and
challenge the legacies of colonialism. The Syilx/Okanagan territory is a diverse
and beautiful landscape of deserts and lakes, alpine forests and endangered grasslands.
We honour the ancestral stewardship of the Syilx/Okanagan People.

Printed in Canada | Printing 10 9 8 7 6 5 4 3 2 1

INTRODUCTION

NNIE RUTH IS
my mother. Well, she is most everybody's mother. She is also a
beloved grandmother and great-grandmother. Born Annie Ruth
Cummings in 1934, in the rural countryside of Booneville, Mississippi, Annie Ruth is the middle child, with an older and
younger brother. She lived her young life on a farm where her
parents were sharecroppers. She picked cotton herself and saw
the underbelly of poverty as well as the day-to-day struggle it
presented in the bodies, emotions, and psyches of those, including herself, who were living in it.

In the midst of these hardships, there were people who lived
an embodied sense of their own inborn nobility, no matter their
lot in life. People who were wise and loving if you let them be,
but mean and nasty if you made them be. These were people
who could have not only a sharp tongue when needed, but a
sharp blade as well, just in case. They knew how to keep their
souls strong and their spirits alive. As a community, they had
common proverbs and sayings – sayings that commented on life
and offered guidance. But those with the gift of gab had unique
ways of expressing their own take on life. Annie Ruth's mother,
Mildred, was one of those people. She could be tough as nails or

soft as cotton. It all depended on how you were with her. Annie Ruth took in what she heard from her mother.

When Mildred was able to leave Mississippi, she moved with her children to Denver, Colorado. Annie Ruth carried within her the folk wisdom she had heard in casual conversations, as well as the words of warning said in confrontations she witnessed. The deep southern vernacular she had been immersed in had become a part of her. Mixed with her unique personality, zest for life, and love of language, Annie Ruth emerged into womanhood with her own way of delivering pithy words of wisdom, which included warnings to keep a person out of trouble, as well as wake-up calls to encourage a person to do better in life than they were doing.

Sparring with her older brother gave her lots of practice in not letting people talk to her *any ol' way*, and helped her to learn what to say if they tried to. She learned how to bluff her way out of a mess, if she could, and to stand her ground in one if she couldn't. *Yes, my brother taught me a lot of stuff – a lot of stuff. I just don't do everything he taught me*, she says with a laugh.

She married a man, John Dell Sharp, who became a Presbyterian minister. They settled in Atlanta, Georgia, with three children of their own. Being a pastor's wife did not stop her from continuing to be the sassy, feisty, and full-spirited woman who was willing to give direct, common-sense advice to anyone whom she thought needed it – no matter their position – including ministers, doctors, lawyers, politicians, and other professional people she would come to know. In fact, her wit, vivacious personality, and sagacious but down-to-earth counsel made her popular wherever she found herself, whether in a grocery store talking to complete strangers or at fancy banquets sitting with dignitaries. She is able to charm and disarm anyone in her sights.

I have captured gems of her thinking and speaking for print because, well, I believe everyone should have an earful of Annie Ruth's truths. Annie Ruth and her sayings are humorous and straightforward, loving but firm, precocious and ultimately precious. They educate, inspire, and get people to think and to become more aware, especially of themselves. And they are filled with love. Sometimes tough love. Annie's Ruth's love. But it is her love of people that allows them to listen, and it is their listening that can produce transformation.

I have seen it with my own eyes. I have seen her ways and her words slowly change people we allowed to live in our home. I have seen it affect neighbours and neighbourhood kids positively. She has had the same effect on people in our church. I have even seen her awaken people whom she would only encounter once. People quickly pick up that not only is she ultimately *for* them, she is rooting for them, even if it may not seem that way at first, in the moment. But this is the way she works her unique magic. And she has worked her magic wherever she has worked: whether as a hospital aid, teacher's assistant, boarding school housemother, homemaker, or retail clerk. No matter where she is, she has always managed to be Annie Ruth. No pretension, no airs. None needed.

When new acquaintances would come over to our home, they came back sooner rather than later, knowing Annie Ruth would wield her agile mind and quick wit to both play with and test them; keeping them on their toes and encouraging them to keep up, if they could. It was a fun time for all.

As of this printing, Annie Ruth (Mom) is 86 years old. She will sometimes flirt for the pure fun of it, but she has no serious intentions having had a beautiful 50-year marriage before my father passed on. Friends still drop by. So do her grandkids with their own kids. Everyone comes by to be doused; baptized all over again with her inimitable love and guidance delivered with humour, brashness, and joy.

I was raised hearing it all. For a long time, I didn't know what I was hearing. I just knew it was *Mom being Mom*. As I grew older, I began to realize that what my mother carried in her was something quite special. It was a unique perspective, and her way of voicing that perspective was becoming increasingly rare in the spoken-word culture that fostered her witticisms and common-sense sayings in the first place. Not only did people not talk this way anymore, many would not understand her expressions without an explanation.

The Deep South, with the many who lived the aftermath of slavery as sharecroppers on the same land they and their ancestors were slaves on, was evolving. Annie Ruth was part of the migration away to the city. But she brought the country truisms with her.

I call her a resurrection woman. She brings people to life. She brings life to life!

It wasn't until I became a writer that I conceived the idea of collecting her sayings. I wanted to preserve what I heard from her in order to share them with others who might appreciate this living art form. I began to write down her sayings. I carried a voice recorder when I went home to visit her in hopes of capturing nuggets of Annie Ruth's truths. I began putting the book together when I counted them one day and realized I had 82 Annie Ruth's truths. Annie Ruth also happened to be 82. I took that as a beautiful sign to begin putting them into a form that could be shared. As I did, I kept adding new ones as they came. Each is a jewel of language and thought, a response to life in the midst of life. Annie Ruth's truths capture heartfelt sentiments that can make you think twice, laugh out loud, or shake your head and say *Hmph!*

There must be many that I missed through the years, taking them for granted because they were part and parcel of my daily life with Annie Ruth. Sometimes I would remember part of a saying and Annie Ruth would fill in the rest. Sometimes she wouldn't remember saying something that I remembered her saying. This was because her statements flowed from her in the moment. What I have captured through my own memory, the memory of others, and the recollection of Annie Ruth herself is now here for your enjoyment, your bemusement and, as Annie Ruth would say, your benefit. I hope you enjoy reading Annie Ruth's truths as much as I have enjoyed collecting them.

1

Annie Ruth's Truth

Be thankful in all things.

MEANING

You don't have to be thankful *for* all things, but you can be thankful *in* all things. This is because within every event of life – even the worst of things – divinity is present. God is there, and therefore so is God's grace, if we care to look for it, no matter how difficult it may be to recognize. There are lessons to learn and there is wisdom to earn in all of life's events. There is compassion to grow into, and ever more powerful insights to realize and to incorporate into life. Being thankful *in* all things helps us to awaken and to see what might be fruitful and useful for our own personal and spiritual growth.

Annie Ruth's Truth

Don't think I don't see. The window is clear on BOTH sides.

MEANING

I see what you're doing just like you see what I'm doing.

A DEEPER MEANING

This is used when someone is trying to be sneaky, surreptitious, or secretive about their activities; when they are trying to hide the truth of their intentions and motives. It is especially useful when someone is being hypocritical by pointing out your faults while not admitting their own.

Annie Ruth's Truth

Even a rooster knows when to crow. How come you don't know?

MEANING

There is a time to speak up and be heard loud and strong. There is also a time to be quiet, a time to be silent.

This is a versatile truth that can be applied to everything from knowing when to boast about something you've done, to knowing when to speak up about an important issue. It can also be said to a person who speaks out of turn or at an inappropriate time.

A DEEPER MEANING

Roosters crow in the morning to announce the rising of the sun. When a person is crowing just to be seen and heard, there's a good chance that it will not only be inappropriate, but that it will be driven by selfishness and ego.

4

Annie Ruth's Truth

Going from pillar to post.

EXAMPLE: Yeah, they're not doing much; just going
from pillar to post, mostly.

MEANING

This is an analogy for people who are not doing much to help
themselves in life. They are, in effect, just going from standing
and leaning against an unmoving pillar to standing and leaning
against an unmoving post. They are engaged in unproductive be-
haviour and fruitless endeavour. In many cases they are just plain
lazy. They are like a pillar or post themselves, because that is about
all the variance and movement the person in question is exhibit-
ing in life. They have no ambition, passion, or drive. Fate is waiting to swallow this kind of person in an abyss of a life not worth
living; one lived without much purpose, direction, or meaning.

ANOTHER MEANING

This saying can also be used for people who are being pushed
around by the circumstances of life; circumstances of which they
are not in control; circumstances that make it very difficult, if
not impossible, to move one's life forward; circumstances where
opportunities are limited and one is effectively trapped.

EXAMPLE: Yes, they are going from pillar to post.
That's about all they can do right now.

Annie Ruth, speaking to me when I'm a teenager.
I'm falling asleep in the living room chair late at night. I don't want to go to bed since there is no school the next day, but I'm obviously sleepy. She encourages me to go to bed *and makes the point this way:*

You will try to sit up as long as that chair, won't you?

After a begrudging acknowledgement of her meaning, I decide to take my mother's advice to go to bed.

6

Acquaintance greeting Annie Ruth,
Hey, Annie Ruth! What's shakin'?

Annie Ruth's Truth

Ain't nothin' shakin' but the leaves on the trees and they wouldn't be shakin' if it wasn't for the breeze.

17

*Annie Ruth is having an intense debate
with a stubborn youth who does not want to hear
the wisdom she is communicating; wisdom that
they sorely need to take in.
Finally, Annie Ruth ends the debate with these words:*

**I don't HAVE to convince you;
I'm just TELLING you.
So there?**

*Annie Ruth telling a young person who is
constantly getting themselves into trouble what
she hopes they might be able to say one day, if they
start to straighten up and do better:*

**I'm not what I want to be ... I'm not
what I ought to be ... but thank God,
I'm not what I was!**

Annie Ruth's Truth

It takes more to be holy than two ears, a nose, and a mouth.

This is spoken to a person or about a person trying to act holier than Thou, who is putting on a show of kindness but is not at all being genuine in their act.

MEANING (IF SPOKEN TO A PERSON DIRECTLY)
I see who you really are. You may be fooling some folk, but you are not fooling me.

MEANING (IF SPOKEN TO SOMEONE ABOUT SOMEONE)
I don't know who they think they're fooling, but they surely are not fooling me.

A DEEPER MEANING
It takes intention, integrity, surrender to the divine, and a sincere commitment of the heart to truly be a good and holy person. If someone is a wolf in sheep's clothing, they will eventually be found out.

Me
Momma, you got some money?

ANNIE RUTH: (WITHOUT HESITATION): I always have dollars, and I have sense *(cents)* with it, too!

I get the message. I then use a complete sentence asking if I can borrow some money.

ANNIE RUTH: Borrow? 'Cause that is what you said, right? You mean, like you're going to pay me back? Because that is still what *borrow* means.

I get the message again. This time I ask if I can *have* a few dollars.

ANNIE RUTH: A few? That is $3 to $5. Is that what you want?

ME (EXASPERATED): Never mind, Mom.

But I got the message, which was …

Annie Ruth's Truth

Ask for what you want.
Be specific. Very specific. Words are important and
what you say matters, because (most) people
aren't mind readers. They only know what you say,
not what you mean. So say what you mean.

Annie Ruth has been babysitting my sister Vanessa's kids.
She receives a phone call from Vanessa telling her that she may be picking up the kids later in the evening than originally planned. Letting Vanessa know, emphatically, that she intends to go to bed at her usual time, and that as tired as she already is, she does not need to be babysitting longer than agreed upon, Annie Ruth says,

Okay, but you need to pick these kids up sooner than later. If you don't, you'll find them on the front steps waiting for you.

Vanessa got the message and came on time.

NOTE: Mom would not have put those kids out on the front steps. She simply didn't want her kindness to be taken advantage of, and she wanted to communicate that emphatically and dramatically. But since you never quite knew for absolute sure what she would or wouldn't do, it was always better not to take a chance, even if you thought she was just bluffing.

Additional Annie Ruth's Truth
I MIGHT JOKE AROUND, BUT I DON'T PLAY!
Also, if you took advantage of her once, it would be the last time. **So, don't make it your first time.**
And that's the Annie Ruth's truth.

Annie Ruth's Truth

The cotton knows how high to grow; and so do you from head to toe.

MEANING

Wisdom is innately present in life. Nature knows what to do without our input. And that includes knowing how tall to grow *you*.

A DEEPER MEANING

Just be grateful that you're alive to grow at all.

*A couple of handymen that were doing yard work and
odd jobs for Annie Ruth one day asked her,*
Can we work overtime?

Annie Ruth

You'd better be glad that you came to work ON time, and that you are working for me ANY time, because you could easily be working for me NO time.

GUYS: Aw, Miss Annie. Why do you say that?

ANNIE RUTH: Because *most* of the time you take too much time. You take too many breaks and you work too slowly. You've taken five hours to do what could have been done in three. I'm paying you to do the *job*, whether it takes you all day or not. I'm not paying you by the hour. How long you take is up to you. I'm just letting you know you aren't getting more money because you took so long. So in my book? You've already been working *overtime!*

NOTE: The guys went back to work and finished the job in short order.

14

Annie Ruth's Truth

The Lord is good, even when bad things happen.

MEANING

Don't blame God for the bad things that happen in life. Misfortune, tragedy, and other pains of life are an unpleasant part of human experience, but God does not cause them. In fact, it is only God, with God's great love for all creation, that can hold all the sorrows, disasters, and heartbreaks of humanity *and* give us the strength to persevere, keep loving, and keep our hope and faith alive.

This is why a person can *be thankful* in *all things*. *(see #1)*

Annie Ruth's Truth

When you move, God moves!

MEANING
Wake up! Do something for yourself! Get going!

A DEEPER MEANING
God helps those who help themselves. If you are just going from pillar to post *(see #4),* being lazy and not trying hard, then don't expect to be blessed. But when you move, then God can work with you. It is your own effort and faith that helps to create the conditions that then allow the graces of life to flow in your direction.

16

Annie Ruth's Truth

You don't have to stay where you started out.

MEANING

You don't have to be stuck. If you have the willpower and courage, you can change your situation, no matter how bad it may seem at the moment. No matter how dismal the outlook.

A DEEPER MEANING

God can make a way out of no way.

Me

Mom, why do you go around humming so much?

Annie Ruth's Truth

Because when you hum the devil don't know what you're talkin' about.

NOTE: Humming carries messages that words cannot convey. It can carry feelings and emotions that words can only approach. Humming allows a person to dive deep into their own soul, to locate and acknowledge their deepest longings and darkest pains. Humming can be a healing balm for life's hurts. It can act as a sacred temple; a time of communion with God, whose grace and love is within the hum itself.

Do you hum?

18

Annie Ruth's Truth

You might hit me one time, but that'll be your last victory – at least with me.

MEANING

I'm going to do whatever I need to do to make sure that the one punch you got lucky enough to hit me with, if you hit me at all, won't happen again. Now, you can take that any way you want to. I'm just warning you.

REAL MEANING

I'm bluffing, but I know what to say!

A DEEPER MEANING

If you hit me, I am going to turn the other cheek. That way, I win even if I lose. How? Holding unconditional love for your challenger or opponent brings an inner victory even if you are tested or bested. This is an example of virtue carrying its own reward.

19

Annie Ruth's Truth

If they won't LET you in, then let YOURSELF in!

Find the key – make the key – *become* the key! Then watch! They will come looking for *you* because they'll realize *you're* the one with the key! And when they ask *How'd you do it?* You can say, *I created myself.*

So don't look around. Look within. Don't look down. Look out! And then tell everybody else to *Look out, 'cause here I come!*

Annie Ruth's Truth

Give people more re-spect than they ex-pect.

21

Annie Ruth's Truth

When people ask me HOW'S LIFE TREATING YOU? I answer that life is treating me just fine.

Then I ask them the same question.
If they start complaining about everything, not saying anything positive about their life and talking about how life is treating them badly, I will ask them,
and how are *you* treating life?
This usually gets people to stop complaining and think a bit, because you tend to reap what you sow.

A DEEPER UNDERSTANDING

Mom always taught us that you tend to get back what you put out in life. If you are kind, you tend to get kindness back. If you are joyful, joy tends to find its way to you. Your outlook on life reflects life right back to you. If you are a loving person you tend to receive love back, and so on. Like attracts like.

How are *you* treating life?

Annie Ruth's Truth

If you can't live life one way, live it another?

MEANING

If doors are closed in one direction, go another direction. If you keep hitting your head against the wall, so to speak, try something else, even if that means you have to go about things very differently than you had planned or hoped. You never know, you might end up right where you want to be. And if not, it might be a better situation than you had imagined. Even if you end up where you want to be later than you wanted, you can say *better late than never*!

A DEEPER TRUTH

Since we do not always know what is best for us, the adventure of life is also an opportunity, at times, to test how much we can surrender and trust the unfolding of life. Even when we have a plan, perhaps we should leave room for the Holy Spirit to change it.

Annie Ruth's Truth

If you chase two rabbits you will lose them both.

MEANING

Pick something and stick with it for a while. If you go in two different directions, you will not be able to give either your full attention or your best effort. You may, in fact, lose them both due to lack of focus and inability to make a choice.

A DEEPER TRUTH

Make the choice you think is best and give it all you've got.

NOTE: Yes, Mom was saying this to me. I am sort of that Renaissance person who likes to do and pursue a lot of different things at the same time. Though I chased even more than two rabbits at a time sometimes, I eventually saw for myself the wisdom of this country proverb. It doesn't mean you can't do more than one thing. It is just a vivid reminder that it may be wiser to concentrate on one thing at a time. Mom never told me which rabbit to focus on, but she did say *God is letting you do all these other things. But at some point you're going to have to do God's work.* I think I am doing that. I still see the other rabbits, but I can enjoy watching them now without needing to chase them. But it was fun while it lasted. At least I wasn't going from pillar to post. *(see #4)*

Me

Mom, I'm realizing there's a lot about you I don't know.

Annie Ruth's Truth

What you don't know about me could make a new world.

Annie Ruth's Truth

Growing up, I didn't have any peer pressure. That's because I pressured the peers!

Annie Ruth's Truth

People start acting like they have some sense when you start acting like you don't.

MEANING

When people are trying to take advantage of you, don't let them. Do whatever you need to do to let them know that *the window is clear on both sides. (see #2)*

A DEEPER MEANING

When you act more a fool than the fool who's trying to fool you, then they tend to come to their senses and act right.

It can also mean that people tend to straighten up and change their actions when they realize you are willing to act *wronger* and longer than they are.

Right. I know *wronger* isn't a word, but in Annie Ruth's world bending the language to make it do what you want it to do is allowed – as long as you *know* that's what you're doing. Otherwise, she will correct your English in a minute *(meaning immediately)*.

27

*Annie Ruth's response to a friend whose
verbal support is less than compassionate
and is more harsh than helping:*

**You're rough enough when
you're on my side. I'd hate to
have you against me.**

28

Annie Ruth's Truth

Look in the mirror.
Now, tell yourself that you
are good at what you do.

But if you aren't, then be honest – and vow to get good!
Then do it. Get good! There is no other way.
Make the sacrifice! Spend the time!
Do the work. And make it fun.
Then, if the opportunity doesn't come, well, you're still good!

(However, see #16)

Annie Ruth's Truth

The reason the world seems to be run by idiots is that it is already being run by a genius, and anyone who seeks to assume that position must be an idiot.

*Annie Ruth to her daughter, who wants to buy a car
that she and her husband are selling:*

I'll let you buy the car from us for 69 dollars a month.

VANESSA: Why 69?

ANNIE RUTH: Well, okay: 169.

VANESSA: Okay, okay! I get the message.
Sixty-nine dollars is just fine.

31

Annie Ruth speaking to a young woman.
The young woman tells her that she is sometimes teased
for her size and weight. Annie tells her,

**If you're a big person and
other people call you fat, say
I MIGHT BE FAT TO YOU, BUT TO ME
I HAD TO CREATE A BODY THAT COULD
HOLD ALL THE LOVE I HAVE INSIDE.
I EVEN HAVE A LITTLE FOR YOU.
See how they like that!**

ANNIE RUTH'S POINT

Don't let them get to you. You get to them. Don't let them bring
you down. You bring them up – with your joy and confidence in
who you are. It may not always be easy, but you can do it.

Annie Ruth counselling a young woman
who has been called ugly:

If folks say that you are ugly, say I MIGHT BE UGLY TO YOU, BUT TO ME? YOU'VE JUST FAILED MY TEST.

See, I chose this face as a test to find that person who can
see my inner beauty, and who is not skin-deep.
When I find that person, I will lavish on them
the treasures of my soul, which are rich and plentiful.
You just missed your chance.
You are NOT the one.
So goodbye!

33

Annie Ruth's Truth

Every day is a good day, even if it's a bad one.

MEANING

At least you're still alive to try to make it better.

A DEEPER MEANING

Count your blessings.

*One day, I was talking with Mom about
the many problems and challenges in the world.*
After a considerable amount of time and debate, we realized
that we were right back where we started. Mom said ...

Annie Ruth's Truth

**If I can't solve the world's problems,
I might as well try to solve my own?
THAT should help the world out
a little bit.**

Annie Ruth's Truth

You can lead a horse to water, but you can't make it drink. You can send a boy to college, but you can't make him think.

MEANING

My mother is one of the smartest people I've ever met, much smarter than many who have *education*. Her point is that a person may have book knowledge, but that doesn't mean they have common sense.

NOTE: The use of the word *boy* instead of *person* reflects the reality of the time she grew up. She encountered many men who thought they knew it all; men driven by arrogance and ego; men she had to *school* in a way they needed but didn't *know* they needed. These were people she realized could use a little humbling, a little guidance; who needed to know they weren't God's gift to everyone and everything just because they were standing there. And, as far as she was concerned, class was *always* in session.

36

Annie Ruth's Truth

Don't forget which side your bread is buttered on!

Usually said as a response to someone she is helping financially in some way, but who is giving her attitude.

MEANING

All right now. Don't forget who is supporting you and has been supporting you!

A DEEPER MEANING

If you don't appreciate what I'm doing for you, you can go right back to where you were before you asked for my help. You had better realize who it is you're talking to now, *'cause I don't play that mess!*

37

Annie Ruth's Truth

If I didn't give it a go, I wouldn't have a go to give.

MEANING

Because I tried, I can try again. But if I didn't try, I couldn't try again because I never tried in the first place.

A DEEPER MEANING

You reap what you sow. You get what you give. What goes around comes around. The more you give, the more you receive, etc.

Annie Ruth's Truth

You are not going to worry my black hair gray.

MEANING

I am not going to get old before my time worrying about you. I am not in control of what you do. Don't expect me to step in and try to save you from yourself when you won't listen to reason or wisdom and seem hell-bent on doing what you want to do even if it is the worst thing for you. Don't come crying to me playing victim when the walls come crashing in – because I have already told you what's going to happen. So there! I'm through with it, because *you are not going to worry my black hair gray!*

*One of Annie Ruth's granddaughters, who is in her 20s,
calls Annie Ruth on the phone complaining
about getting older:*
Maw-maw *(the granddaughter's pet name for Annie Ruth),*
I don't want another birthday.

Annie Ruth's Truth

Well, you better. Because not having one means you'll be dead.

GRANDDAUGHTER (A LITTLE TAKEN ABACK):
Uhhh … Okay then. Thanks, Maw-maw.

ANNIE RUTH: You're welcome. Call anytime.

410

Annie Ruth's Truth

It's easy to forget the easiest things to remember.

Annie Ruth's Truth

Folks treat you better if they know you have another place else to go.

This is the reason Mom never let our home be sold when Dad was offered a job as a pastor that came with a manse.

And yes, she said *another place else*, instead of *someplace else*. It is so incorrect that it makes wonderful, joyful sense, while making, even more emphatically, the point about how important it is to have your own home. That way, she says, you don't have to be beholden to anyone, no matter what happens with a job.

NOTE: As a former English teacher, I have always enjoyed how Mom, herself a lay English teacher, plays with language.

42

*Annie Ruth and a brother-in-law are having fun
teasing each other on the phone long distance.
The brother-in-law's wife overhears their banter and gets
on the phone, saying to Annie Ruth,*
Why do you let him talk to you like that?

Annie Ruth's Truth

**You have to put up with it E-VER-Y DAY.
You LIVE with the man. I, on the
other hand, can hang up on him
AN-Y-TIME I want to.**

Annie Ruth on her 81st birthday.
She is out to lunch with some members of the family,
including her two daughters, their husbands, and
their children (her grandchildren).

Annie Ruth's Truth

**Uh oh ... the sun is shining?
I'm dangerous now. 'Cause when the
sun is shining it makes me feel GOOD?
And it makes me want to act up.
So y'all better WATCH OUT NOW?**

An Annie Ruth's poetic thingamajig:

**Grandma Gray, may I go out to play?
No my child, it's too rainy a day?
A man came along and said
it's a pretty day to play.
Take three licks and go to
your room and stay.**

MEANING

This innocent and simple sounding poem is about keeping a child safe from potential danger or abuse. It harkens back to the notion of obeying your elders without talking back or questioning why. Sometimes parents didn't have time to explain their strictness in the moment. They just needed the child to do what they said, immediately and in silence. The innocence and trusting nature of children was held in the wisdom and worldly knowing of those loving parents and guardians who protected and cared for them.

Annie Ruth was known to cook up a storm on Sundays.
She loved preparing a traditional southern soul food dinner, with so many choices it was sometimes hard to keep up with them. Unless there was company, it was usually done in a buffet style, where everything was either on the stove or on a serving table.

One Sunday, upon sitting down at the dinner table, my sister saw that I had some food she didn't have.

CELANESE: Wait! David, you have some okra? Mama, where's the okra?

ANNIE RUTH: On David's plate.

NOTE: Mom would make these kinds of obviously annoying statements just to see how we would respond. It was her way of seeing what was in us, how we responded to life in the moment, and what we would say to give life a run for its money, so to speak. It was this kind of verbal give-and-take that allowed Mom to see what our inner strength was like. If we were able to respond with our own strength, she would either keep going to see if we could, or say, *all right now, show me something!* As an acknowledgment that she liked our response and strength of spirit.

She knew life was going to test us, so she tested us first.

Annie Ruth cut her finger while opening a can of green beans.
I helped patch her up, as she didn't want to go to the doctor for possible stitches – not on this Sunday, as she was in the midst of cooking a grand Sunday meal for everybody, including those from the church who just might stop by.

My sisters found out about the incident and called to see how she was. When my youngest sister, Celanese, got her on the phone, we put the conversation on the speaker. Celanese kept on talking and asking questions until Annie Ruth finally said, with attitude,

I'm done with you now. I got to go finish cooking.

CELANESE: *That's* what I was waiting for – that Annie Ruth attitude! Now I *know* you're okay and I can hang up in peace.

ANNIE RUTH, SURPRISED AND IMPRESSED WITH THIS SHOW OF VERBAL PLAY CHIMED BACK: *All right now. Show me something!*

Annie Ruth telling me about an incident that occurred during her high school days:

I remember one time my brother Elvester and I were at a dance and a boy said to him, *Hey, man, you almost stepped on my foot.*

Elvester responded, *Well, put your damn foot in your pocket.*

The boy's face got that who-do-you-think-you're-talkin'-to look. As the boy was about to say something back, Elvester hit him, *WHOPP!!* and knocked him out!

I asked Mom, *And what did you do? Did you ask why he did that?*

ANNIE RUTH: Naw, 'cause I knew how he was. I just said, ***What took you so long?***

48

Annie Ruth, 80, is sitting in her favourite
lounge chair in the den, asleep.
My sister Vanessa bends down over Annie Ruth's shoulder to kiss
her on the cheek. Suddenly, Annie Ruth delivers a left hook to
Vanessa's right temple. Surprised and dazed, Vanessa says, I
thought you were asleep!

Annie Ruth's Truth

**I was. But you forget that I was
Annie Ruth Cummings before I
became Annie Ruth Sharp.
And when I'm asleep and you sneak
up on me, even to kiss me, you are
gambling and are bound to meet
Annie Ruth Cummings –
and her fist?**

Vanessa never made that mistake again.

*Mom and I were discussing a present I bought her
online and sent for her 81st birthday.*
It was a jar of little notes, each in their own little envelope. There were 31 of them. She could open one each day and make her birthday last a whole month. Since I only saw pictures of the gift I ordered, I had a question for her.

ME: I couldn't tell from the picture … How tall is the jar?

ANNIE RUTH: Oh, I don't know.

ME: Well, is it a foot tall?

ANNIE RUTH: Whose foot?

I was preparing to drive with Annie Ruth
to the grocery store.
It was a cool but not too cold sunny winter's day.
Annie Ruth was all bundled up in a heavy jacket,
thick scarf, knit cap, and gloves. I asked her,
Why are you so bundled up?

Annie Ruth's Truth

I don't mind being out in the cold.
I just don't want to be cold
while I'm out.

Annie Ruth, 80, on a phone call from an old friend from high school she hasn't heard from in many years.

FRIEND: How are you, Annie?

Annie Ruth's Truth

I'm alive ... I'm alive!!
Still kicking ... but not high!

*Celanese, newly single again, was lamenting
the amount of weight she felt she needed to lose to
attract someone new. Annie Ruth sought to make her
feel less stressed about it all and said,*

Nobody likes a bone but a dog.

MEANING

Don't worry so much. Someone will like you just the way you
are, for just the way you are, for the meat that's on your bones!
And she was right. And it didn't take long.

Annie Ruth, 83-years-young, was on the phone
telling me about her present state of walking,
due to a knee that is giving her problems.
She explained how she was helped to her car after church
with her cane in one hand while she held on to the
shoulder of a helper with her other hand.

With great joy, she said to me,

I was telling my helper ... In my younger years I was always standing straight and being independent. Now? I'm leaning and depending?

She explained,

I'm LEANING on the Lord and DEPENDING on God's grace.

I am shopping at the local pharmacy
with Annie Ruth.
Seeing the greeting card section and knowing how
she likes to send cards to people, I say, Mom, did you
want to pick up some cards while we're here?

Annie Ruth's Truth

I don't pick UP cards.
I pick OUT cards.

Annie Ruth loves playing with the exactness of words and help-ing people become more aware of their own word choices. Being a writer, Mom loved catching me using words that didn't quite fit the bill.

This particular difference in word choice was her way to engage me in a conversation on how much she enjoys finding greeting cards specific to the person, the personality, and the situation.

So we picked *out* cards.

A hot dog vendor working the stands at
a baseball game holds up his offering and shouts,
Hey, hot dogs! ... HEY, HOT DOGS!

Annie Ruth shouts back,

I don't like HAY in my hot dogs!
I like meat in mine!

The crowd around her laughed and shouted their joy at her
quick-witted response. She had just hit a home run.

I'm calling Annie Ruth, 81, on her cell phone:
Hi, Mom!

ANNIE RUTH: Oh! Hi there!

ME: I'm just calling to check in on you.

ANNIE RUTH: Well, I'm checking out.

ME: What?

ANNIE RUTH: You called to check *in*, but I'm about to check *out*.

ME (JUST A BIT CONCERNED NOW): Mom, where are you? Are you all right?

ANNIE RUTH: I'm in line at the grocery store and I'm at the cashier now, about to check *out*.

ME (RELIEVED): Oh ... Okay, I see now. You got me, Mom.

ANNIE RUTH (LAUGHING): Well, thanks for checking in. I'll check *you* out later.

ME (TRYING TO KEEP UP): Okay, Mom. I guess I'm checking out now too, then.

ANNIE RUTH: Well, you can check out. Just don't die on me.

ME: Uhh … I'm just leaving, that's all.

ANNIE RUTH: Well, you can leave me, just don't forget me.

ME: As if anyone could. Okay. Bye, Mom.

ANNIE RUTH: *Buy* yourself; I'm not for sale!

ME: So long, Mom!

ANNIE RUTH: But not too long, now … but not too soon, either.

ME: MOM! Okay, I promise.

ANNIE RUTH: Don't make promises you can't keep, now.

ME: Mom, you are incredulous. Aren't you checking *out*? I will check *in* with you later.

ANNIE RUTH (LAUGHING): Okay, you do that. **And don't call me incredulous. Call me incredible!**

ME (SHAKING MY HEAD): Okay, you are incredibly incredulous.

ANNIE RUTH (APPROVING MY COMEBACK): All right now! Show me something!

One year, Mom sent me a Father's Day gift. It was a cheque for $100 plus a $1 bill. Of the dollar bill, she wrote on a note,

Have an ice cream cone or two!

I called to thank her for the thoughtful gift and playfully informed her that ice cream cones were considerably more expensive now. I also informed her that I had picked up the mail not knowing what was inside the letter. I then proceeded to put the mail down and make an ice cream cone, which I had not done in many months. I said, Mom, there must be some mystical connection happening with us. It is really *cool* that I was making an ice cream cone while having just received your letter, still unopened, which urged me to get an ice cream cone.

ANNIE RUTH: Well, ice cream is *cool* ... Get it?

ME: Yes, ma'am. I got it all right.

ANNIE RUTH: Well, since you *got* it, I guess you can eat it, which means you don't need my dollar for ice cream. So you can go ahead and send that dollar back ... But keep the hundred.

*Annie Ruth is on the phone talking to a telemarketer,
who is trying to convince her why she needs to buy whatever
they are selling. But Mom usually frustrates them.*

This can turn out to be very entertaining for her; especially when
they realize she is not a pushover. Usually, she tries to end the
conversation nicely, not wanting to be rude, but letting the person know she is not going to buy what they are trying to sell.

On this occasion, the salesperson was not giving up so easily. Mom, who loves a challenge, was not about to give in to something she knew she didn't want to buy. The caller didn't know
yet who it was they were dealing with. Mom practically had tears
in her eyes from laughing quietly while looking at me and talking to the salesperson. Finally, she stops talking back and forth
and listens to a lengthy sales pitch. I knew that the salesperson
was probably gaining hope and confidence because Mom was
listening so quietly. I also knew she was setting the salesperson
up for a letdown; I just didn't know how it would come out.

After the sales pitch has been completed, Mom responded
with this Annie Ruth's Truth.

You can TELL me anything, but you can't make me BELIEVE anything.

*The salesperson, exasperated, gave up and hung up. Mom, with a smile
on her face, looked over at me and winked. She said,* I bet they won't
be calling *me* again.

A friend was telling Annie Ruth about a service
he was offering that wasn't attracting customers.
It seems he had overpriced his services. Annie Ruth
was talking to him about lowering his prices.

Annie Ruth's Truth

It's better to have AIRN than NAIRN.

MEANING
It's better to have some earnings than no earnings.

TRANSLATION
airn = earnings
nairn = no earnings

NOTE: The language is being stretched and bended, played with
while being infused with emotional pliability. This kind of folk
poetry is filled with humour as well as common sense. It is why
I have sought to collect these sayings. It is not only for my recollection and enjoyment, but also for the enjoyment of anyone who
can appreciate what they are being treated to.

Annie Ruth to a friend
How are things going for you these days?

FRIEND: Well, I have more time than money.

Annie Ruth's Truth

You don't know that. You might know how much money you have, but you don't know how much time you have. You could go right now.

FRIEND (SOMEWHAT THROWN OFF): Well, I guess I never thought about it like that.

ANNIE RUTH (WITH HER TRADEMARK SMILE): That's why I'm here!

Me to Annie Ruth, after a lengthy
conversation about life and love:
I love you, Mom.

Annie Ruth's Truth

**I love you, too. I can't tell you
how much I love you, but I can
tell you I love you MUCH!**

Annie Ruth answering a friend's query
as to how she is doing:

Annie Ruth's Truth

I'm fine as wine
and really on the ball.
No windows and no doors —
just a hole in the wall.

MEANING

The first two lines are easily understood. *I'm doing all right; more than all right. Actually, I am doing great!* But those last two lines?

Some background: I had no idea about this analogy. Mom explained that it had to do with what were called juke joints. Where she was from, some of these places were built with no doors or windows. They only had a hole in the wall for people to come through.

A DEEPER MEANING

This connection to juke joints makes the poetic response rich in what it communicates. Juke joints were places to relax and have fun. They were places to let it all hang out, to dance and drink, to forget about your troubles for a while. In this respect, the poem is expressing that the person is in a good place, that they are not so burdened by life, and that right now life is good!

A neighbour stops by Annie Ruth's house one evening.
Hey, Mrs. Sharp!

ANNIE RUTH: Hey yourself, Henry! What brings you over?

HENRY: Well, I can smell your cookin' from 'cross the street.
Sure smells good, too. I thought I'd come over and
see if you're done?

ANNIE RUTH (UNDERSTANDING CLEARLY WHAT HE WANTS):
Oh. Well, I'm done two ways.

HENRY: Done two ways? What do you mean?

Annie Ruth's Truth

DONE cooked it. DONE ate it up.

Henry went back home, disappointed.

*Annie Ruth to a friend who came by for
a short visit one evening:*

Hey now! You are looking good. Did you go out tonight?

FRIEND: Yeah, but I spent too much money.

ANNIE RUTH: Did you have any fun?

FRIEND: Well, yeah … a little, I guess.

Annie Ruth's Truth

Hmm … but it sounds like you had more spending than fun.

*You should have taken me!
That would have guaranteed you having more fun than
spending 'cause you know how much fun I am and you
know I would have saved you from spending
all that money you spent.*

NOTE: Not that Annie Ruth would have gone or have even *wanted* to go. She was simply making a point. And sometimes that *is* the point.

Annie Ruth, being the generous great-grandmother, grandmother, and mother that she is, invited the kids, the grandkids, and the great-grandkids over for one of her famous Sunday dinners.

She cooked enough for an army, but no one came. They all had some reason or another for not showing up. However, as life would have it, several friends just happened to stop by randomly. (Perhaps not so randomly, as many knew she liked to cook a lot on the weekends, just in case anyone stopped by.)

Of course, they smelled the food and wondered if they were in time to eat. The answer was Yes!

After everyone had come and gone, there was hardly any food left. Annie Ruth decided to make a list of what she had cooked:

cornbread

fried corn (half whole kernel, half cream style, mixed together)

boiled cabbage, green beans, and potatoes (mixed together)

rice

salad

candied yams

okra

corn on the cob

neck bones

baked chicken

black-eyed peas

macaroni and cheese

greens (turnips and mustards mixed)

When I called from California and heard this story, I said, Mom, I'm not used to you writing down what you cooked. Why did you make a written menu?

Annie Ruth's Truth

So that when I get a phone call from all of those who didn't come over today, asking about coming over tomorrow to eat, I can tell them what they won't be getting.

Annie Ruth called her brother-in-law to wish him a happy birthday. When he answered the phone, she sang a joyous and lively rendition of the song to him. Afterwards, the brother-in-law, who loves to tease and spar with Annie Ruth said,

Uh, well ... Thanks for singing, Annie. But don't quit your day job.

He started laughing, thinking he had scored a verbal victory and left Annie Ruth speechless. But Annie Ruth, without hesitation, immediately replied,

This IS my day job!

It was the brother-in-law who was left speechless.

67

A friend of Annie Ruth (81) was planning a party.
The friend was a good 20 years younger than Annie Ruth. The friend told Annie Ruth she was going to start the party at 7:00 p.m. and hoped Annie Ruth would come and bring some of her pals as well. Annie Ruth replied that she and the women she would bring were too old for 7:00 p.m. parties. She told her friend that she needed to be home before it got dark, and that she would be in bed by 9:00. She suggested that if her friend really wanted her and her friends to be there, then she should start the party at 5:00. The friend exclaimed, Five o'clock …!?

Annie Ruth's Truth

Yes. That way we can come to your party and stay awhile – even if we're leaving while everyone else is coming!

Annie Ruth answers a knock on the door.

She sees through the door window that it is a former high school classmate of mine. This former classmate has not had it easy in life. He has been walking up and down the neighbourhood streets for many years. He is in his late 50s, is always dishevelled, and talks to himself constantly. Annie is used to him knocking on her door asking for a handout. Annie Ruth opens the door ...

MAN: Hi, Mrs. Sharp. How you doing?

ANNIE RUTH: I'm fine. How are you?

MAN: Okay, okay. How's David?

ANNIE RUTH: He's doing just fine.

MAN: Okay, okay. That's good. Glad to hear it. Mrs. Sharp ... can I get something to eat or a little change?

ANNIE RUTH: Not today. You caught me at a bad time, right now.

MAN: Oh, okay then. Well, can I get a hug?

ANNIE RUTH: You want a hug? Well, I'd give you a hug, but I don't like the way you smell. And I don't want that smell on me.

Come back sometime when you've taken a bath and have cleaned yourself up; and then maybe I'll give you a hug.

The man comes back the next day! And he is cleaned up and smelling good!

ANNIE RUTH: Hey, hey, HEY! I guess you want a hug *today!*

And yes, she gave him a hug. And some food. And a little change. And a message.

ANNIE RUTH: Now don't come back here tomorrow thinking I'm going hug you every day.

MAN: Oh, yes ma'am.

Annie Ruth's Truth

You need to clean up for yourself. You keep it up then maybe somebody else will hug you, too!

*The same man looking for a handout on another day says,
Mrs. Sharp, will you lend me some money?*

ANNIE RUTH: Now, listen. I can't *lend* money to somebody
that doesn't have a job.

MAN: Well, then can you *give* me some money?

ANNIE RUTH (APPRECIATING THAT HE'S GOT ENOUGH
SPUNK TO PLAY HER GAME): *Now that I can do!*

*Annie Ruth talking to one of the guys that
comes to work for her. After he has done his work,
Annie Ruth pays him and gives him some food
to take with him. He says,*
Mrs. Sharp, I like working for you.

Annie Ruth's Truth

**Everybody likes working for me,
'cause I pay 'em and I feed 'em.
I'd like working for me, too?**

Annie Ruth's son-in-law came to visit one day and
complained that his hip was beginning to hurt.
Annie suggested maybe he needed a hip replacement.

The son-in-law then inquired about Annie Ruth's right knee, which has been hurting for some time. He knew that doctors had told her she should think about having a replacement operation herself, so he asked her whether she was going to have one.

Annie Ruth's Truth

No, no! I'm 83 years old. I will keep my knees. I can see it now. I get a new knee and then die soon after. I'll tell you what, though. If I did get a new knee and that happened, y'all had better open up the coffin so everybody can take a good look at my good knee!

*Annie Ruth has been getting two to four phone calls daily
for over 30 years from a man.*

He is a former high school friend of Annie Ruth's daughter,
Vanessa. He was injured in a motorcycle accident while in high
school and sustained some brain damage. Confined to a wheel-
chair, he reaches out to anyone who will spend time with him on
the telephone.

One day, after many years, the man asked Annie Ruth,
How come you never call me?

Annie Ruth's Truth

**Because! You call me so much
that you don't give me a chance to call
you. You only give me the chance to
tell you to stop calling me so much.**

73

*A relative stops by the house. Annie Ruth, known for
her good cooking, offers food as a polite gesture.*
Would you like something to eat while you're here?

RELATIVE: Oh, yes!

ANNIE RUTH: Don't you ever say, *No?*

RELATIVE: No.

Annie Ruth's Truth

Well, then I might have to say NO for you, sometime. Not only to keep you from eating up all my food when you "stop by," but to keep you out of trouble when you DON'T stop by.

NOTE: She said this last line to people who were going down a
path that was not positive. She would encourage them to make
better choices using her sense of humour, even though she was
serious. If the message didn't get through, she would tell them
directly what they needed to hear. You didn't want it to get to
that point because she could point her finger in a way that was
like a magic wand, and tell you about yourself and where you
were going wrong and where you were going to end up if you
didn't straighten up. Then she would straighten her finger and
say, *You hear me, now, don't you!?*

The answer was always *Yes, ma'am.*

*Annie Ruth, as a house mom at a boarding school,
said this to a young woman she caught trying to
sneak out of the dorm past curfew:*

You're not so slick that you can't stand another greasing!

MEANING

You're not as clever as you think you are.

75

I had come to visit Annie Ruth for a week.

I came into the kitchen one evening after dinner and went to give her a hug while she was drying dishes. She happened to be drying a very sharp knife at the time. As I leaned in to kiss her, she matched my lean, moving the knife up to my neck at the same speed, and said, slowly,

You are VER-Y trusting.

I backed away laughing
and blew her a kiss instead.

One night when my father, Rev. John Sharp, was away attending a church conference, Annie Ruth's brother showed up at the house and knocked on the door. It was 4:00 in the morning. Annie Ruth, startled, went to the door and yelled, Who is it?

BROTHER: It's your brother, Elvester!

ANNIE RUTH: What are you doing knocking on my door at four in the morning? What do you want?!

BROTHER: I just want ten dollars, that's all.

ANNIE RUTH (REALIZING HER BROTHER IS INEBRIATED AND POSSIBLY EVEN HIGH ON SOMETHING): Oh, wait a minute! You want ten dollars from me at four in the morning, after waking me up from my good night's sleep? Okay, hold on. I'll be right back.

Annie Ruth went away. When she came back she opened the door. In her hand was a pistol. She waved it in her brother's face. What did you say you wanted?

Her brother was startled! He had known his sister all her life, but this surprised him, especially since she had been a preacher's wife for some time. He said to a friend who had come along,

Come on, man! We gotta leave before she shoots us. And that's my sister! Let's go!!

One day, I called Mom a number of times. Each time, the
answering machine came on right away. Concerned, I called
back later. When she realized it was me, she said,
Oh, hi. What's going on?

ME: I called you a number of times earlier, but you didn't answer.

ANNIE RUTH: Oh, that must have been when some telemarketer
called me. I didn't want to talk to them, but I didn't just want to
hang up on them either. But when I told them I didn't want to
talk to them, they just kept talking. So I just put the phone down
on the table. But before I did, I told them,

**Listen, I have things to do, and
you won't be polite and let me go
without me hanging up on you.
So, you can keep talking if you
want to, but I'm leaving. You didn't
think I was just sitting around here
waiting for you to call, did you?**

And then I put the phone down on the table
and went on about my business.

Annie Ruth was invited to come to an event. She declined because it would end at night. She told her inviter,

I don't want to be stranded at night.

After a moment's hesitation she offered,

I don't mind being stranded in the daytime though.

*Annie Ruth wearing several layers of clothes to church,
knowing the heat hasn't been working. Someone asks her,*
How many layers are you wearing?

Annie Ruth's Truth

**Don't you worry about it, none.
I'm wearing enough to keep me warm,
but not enough to lend.
Enough to keep the cold at bay and let
the heat stay in.
Enough to let the Spirit through to
melt what's still cold-hearted.
Enough to make it through this chilly
service if we ever get started!**

That was a sermon in and of itself!

I arrived on a Saturday to visit Annie Ruth for a week.
After unpacking and settling in, I reminded her that
I would be with her until Friday. Annie Ruth pointed
her finger at me and gave a playful warning:

Maybe.

Her point?
She would determine whether I actually completed my stay.

81

*Annie Ruth telling me about an experience
her own mother had:*

My mom, Mildred, was visiting a friend who was cooking dinner. She noticed that her friend had a cold and that her nose was
runny, with one nostril dripping down to her lip. The friend,
who was stirring a pot of greens and attending to the fried chicken,
was unaware of the drip. She asked my mom if she was staying
for dinner. Momma said to the woman,

Depends on how the drop falls.

NOTE: Now you see where Annie Ruth got the inspiration for
her own truths. This mixture of humour and pithy wisdom
helped keep people sane and hopeful in adverse circumstances.

A man telephoned Annie Ruth.
In an intimidating and gruff voice, he said,
Uhh ... Yes. I need to speak to ... uhh ...
Annie ... R ... uhh ... Sharp.

ANNIE RUTH (PICKING UP THE TENOR OF THIS CALL): Uhh ... Yes. You are speaking to ... uhh ... Annie ... R ... uhh ... Sharp.

MAN: Well, I'm calling ... Annie ... because I want you to know that ... uhhh... you owe ...

ANNIE CUT THE MAN OFF: Listen, I don't know who you are, but I don't owe *an-y*-body *an-y*-thing! You hear me? In fact, people owe *me!*

MAN: Ma'am, I am not going to debate this with you.

ANNIE RUTH: Good. Then I'm not going to debate with you either. But I will 'cause I'm a good debater.

MAN: Bye.

Annie Ruth's Truth

Buy yourself! I'm not for sale!

A man who has been doing handyman work for Annie Ruth for more than a decade and who is barely making ends meet from month to month, attended a Thanksgiving Day gathering at her home, along with several other people. Annie Ruth has helped this man in many ways, but in the process has also had to deal with his pride and ego. As the group held hands, Annie Ruth invited each person to say a few words of thanks.

The handyman offered these heartfelt words:

I thank God for this woman ... Mrs. Sharp. I really don't know what I'd do without her. I really don't.

Annie Ruth couldn't help chiming in,

I thank God for you, too ... uhhh ... most of the time.

Everyone burst out laughing and the solemn prayer time was *over*.

*Annie Ruth sees one of her handymen sitting under a tree
in the backyard. He has escaped the sun, but the heat is about
to be turned up. He is being lazy on a job she is paying him to do.
She goes outside and with arms folded and her head cocked
a little to the side she delivers one of her truths:*

You've got it made in the shade ... until somebody cuts the tree down.

MEANING

The tree is metaphorical. Annie Ruth means she can change the handyman's situation, thinking that he's got it easy, by firing him on the spot. And, in that case, *she* would be the *somebody* that is cutting down the proverbial tree.

He went right back to work.

Annie Ruth and I were discussing someone of prominence who is doing good work in the world now.

It was not always the case for that person. They had lived a life that had hurt a lot of people; a life that had brought scandal on themselves, and eventually jail time for the crimes they had committed. I made a comment about how much older the person looked now, about how much their face had changed. I wondered out loud at how a person can age so drastically.

Annie Ruth's Truth

It's not always what you do.
It's what you DID.

MEANING

It's not always what you do *now* that makes you look older; it's what you did *then*.

A DEEPER MEANING

We don't escape our darker past unscathed. Even when you turn your life around, your body may carry souvenirs from the past, some wear and tear from a life once lived as the price paid for one's past indulgences and misdeeds.

Friend
How are you doing, Annie?

ANNIE RUTH: My knee is hurting. I think I have knee-monia.

FRIEND: You mean *pneu*-monia?

Annie Ruth's Truth

I said my KNEE was hurting, not my lungs. So I have KNEE-monia ... 'cause my KNEE is MOANIN'.

Annie Ruth's Truth

Take the current while it serves.

MEANING
Go with the flow while the flow is good.

A DEEPER MEANING
There is grace in life. In the context of this truth, it is a wave of goodness that embraces you and carries you forward. When you feel that grace, or see things falling into place without much effort on your part, don't fight it. Go with it, for therein you go with God.

And let gratitude be your response.

Leaving a group of close friends after an outing,
Annie Ruth says,
Goodbye. I'll plant you now and dig you later!

Everybody, in their own way, expressed amusement at this corny but creative phrase. Somebody asked,

How do you come up with this stuff?

Annie Ruth's Truth

I don't know if I come up with it or it just comes down to me.

You can take this two ways:
It comes down to her in a mystical way, or
It simply comes down to Annie Ruth being Annie Ruth.

What do you think?

I call Annie Ruth on the phone.
Mom, what are you doing?

Annie Ruth

Oh, I'm watching television in the den. But I'm getting ready to go to bed. After I wash up and check my blood pressure, I'll turn the TV on in the bedroom

and find something to watch ME while I'm asleep.

An Annie Ruth's Truth verbal thingamajig

Whatcha know, Joe?
I don't know nothin'?
Whatcha KNOW, Joe?
I don't know NOTHIN'?
What DO you KNOW, Joe??
I DON'T KNOW NOTHIN'?
So tell me something, 'cause
I DON'T KNOW!

MEANING

This is simply a way of asking someone what's going on. Their response is saying, *I don't know. You tell me.* People who knew this little wordplay would do it in rhythm. It could be done between two people, but also could be spoken as a group chant with one group being Joe and the other group asking Joe *Whatcha know?*

91

Annie Ruth's Truth

You've got eight fingers and two thumbs; you'll go when the wagon comes.

MEANING

You might think you're all high and mighty, but you're just a human being like everybody else. You are no more special than me, or anybody. So get off your high horse and come on back down to earth.

A DEEPER MEANING

When it's your turn to die, you'll go, too. You've got eight fingers and two thumbs; you'll go when the wagon comes. The wagon will come to pick you up and take you to the grave just like it does for everyone else around here.

NOTE: Remember, many of these sayings are born from the warp and woof of country living in the rural south of Mississippi.

Annie Ruth's Truth

You can tell a genius, but you can't tell them much.

This comment was precipitated by a sign I had on my bedroom door when I was in high school. It was a sign that proclaimed I was a genius. It didn't stay up very long. Even as I claimed a brilliance of mind, it became clear that I still had much to learn about most everything. I did, however, keep the sign in a more private location to inspire me from time to time.

93

Annie Ruth's Truth

It's hard but it's fair. You had a good home, but you didn't stay there.

MEANING

This is something Annie Ruth says she heard from a military drill sergeant. It was part of the mental training and adjustment to help – or push – young soldiers to grow up, because *You're in the army now!*

Annie Ruth used this line on me and my sisters as we got older, to remind us that we left home to explore our destinies and live our own lives.

As we transitioned to the world of adult living, my sisters and I would either call or come home for support, rest, and to receive the special nourishment – both food and spirit – that a loving mother can give a child.

Annie Ruth reminded us that life can be hard, but we must keep on keeping on (mostly because we couldn't live there anymore). However, both my sisters *did* move back and live with her during turning points, to help their lives move forward. This was the alternative to the one step forward, two steps backward that happens too often for too many people. This returning home to live with Annie Ruth was one step backward to make a big leap of faith forward.

Though she was happy to have you, she made it clear that it was a temporary situation. For emphasis, she added *A tem-po-ra-ry situation.* Then she made sure by asking, *You hear me, don't ya? (see #73)*

94

Annie Ruth's Truth

Every shut eye ain't sleep and every goodbye ain't gone.

MEANING

Just because you think no one is around who can hear or see you doesn't mean it's true. So be careful and wise. You think you are getting away with something 'cause people were sleep or you thought they had left, but *every shut eye ain't sleep and every goodbye ain't gone*. Just remember that.

NOTE: This is probably my favourite Annie Ruth's truth. But that could change, depending on mood and circumstances. Anyway, there is a wonderful metre to this one. It also lends itself to plenty of *attitude*.

*Annie Ruth, 83, decided she was no longer going to cook
so much for everybody after the next Sunday's get together.*
She said that since her children's children have children now,
it was time someone else started doing what she had been
doing for so many years. This is what she said:

Annie Ruth's Truth

I hope you enjoy this dinner, 'cause it's the last button on Gabriel's coat. Now, put that in your pipe and smoke it.

MEANING

I am done doing what I've been doing.

A DEEPER MEANING

Gabriel, the archangel, is wearing a beautiful coat. Before he blows his horn to call the righteous to heaven, he buttons it. The last button signifies that he has done all he can as an angel of the Lord, for the people of earth. His privileged work and mission have come to an end and the horn is ready to sound the culminating event.

Annie Ruth was sounding her own horn, announcing the coming end to a major life mission of her work in the world. The dinner was the culminating event.

Annie Ruth's Truth

You didn't call any name, so you can't bear any blame.

MEANING

This proverb has to do with accusing someone of wrongdoing. If a person is asked *What happened?* by someone in authority, telling the general story without identifying the perpetrator, allows the person to escape blame for getting anyone in trouble.

This allows the person to be helpful to the authorities while not seeming to implicate the wrongdoer, which keeps the person from incurring their wrath.

Annie Ruth's Truth

People don't believe fat meat is greasy 'til it's fried.

MEANING

This little line is a powerful truth-teller about people who are wolves in sheep's clothing. Sometimes people look good, talk good, and seem good, until they get found out and are put on the hot seat. Then you can see how greasy they really are! Slick on the outside – but greasy on the inside! *(see #74)*

EXAMPLE: I knew that person was a liar. But they sure did have everybody fooled. I knew it was gonna take someone who wasn't afraid of them to confront them in public, 'cause *people don't believe fat meat is greasy 'til it's fried.*

Annie Ruth's Truth

If you can't be good, be careful.

If you need this one explained,
then you need to be *extra* careful.

Annie Ruth's Truth

You may not know this, but you have a bird's nest on the ground.

MEANING

You have an opportunity in easy reach.

EXAMPLE: You don't seem to realize how close you are to a blessing that is just for you. Don't you see it? It's right there! Just get it! Look! It's right there at your feet, practically. You don't have to climb or reach high or work for it. It is being given to you; practically handed to you! Don't you see it!? Well, I see it and I am telling you to claim your blessing and go get those opportunity eggs, 'cause *you have a bird's nest on the ground!*

100

Annie Ruth's Truth

You're a day late and a dollar short!

MEANING

You missed out on something.

Annie Ruth's Truth

I want you lookin' at me at all times. I may not be good-lookin' but I'm gonna be lookin' good!

MEANING

Though this saying seems to be self-deprecating, it is usually only said by someone who already knows they are good-looking. It is a playful boast, where the second line sets up the third line. The third line, a payoff line, should be said with great emphasis and dramatic expression. Switching the words *good* and *lookin'* becomes another wonderful example of wordplay.

Annie Ruth's Truth

Don't be sorry. Apologize, but don't be sorry.

MEANING

To call someone *sorry* is to say they are weak and incompetent. If a person said *I'm sorry* to Annie Ruth, she would invariably let them know this Annie Ruth's Truth.

A DEEPER MEANING

This is a way Annie Ruth encourages people to claim more inner strength. To say *I'm sorry* feeds a negative connotation of ineptness. To say *I apologize* carries with it a stronger energy, where one retains more dignity while admitting a wrongdoing or mistake. It acknowledges that as humans we make mistakes. However, we are also strong, noble beings made in God's image, with dignity and grace, blessed to be, and kissed by the Creator.

We are not *sorry* people!

103

Annie Ruth's Truth

I can teach it to you, but I can't learn it for you.

MEANING

Annie Ruth said this when trying to convey a life lesson to someone who was making the same mistake over and over. They would seek her out for her advice and, if she saw that they weren't actually receiving the needed wisdom because of denial or some other block, she would deliver this Annie Ruth's Truth as a final warning if they wanted to change their life for the better.

Annie Ruth's Truth

No better for ya. SUFFER!

MEANING

This is like saying *You got what you deserved!* It also serves as a wake-up call and implicitly adds the sentiment *If you had listened to me in the first place, you could have avoided all of this. But since you went ahead and did what* you *wanted to do instead of what you* should *have done, then* no better for ya. Suffer! *Maybe* that's *how you need to learn.*

It is important to remember that although Annie Ruth is a kind, compassionate woman, she is well aware that you reap what you sow. She would utter this statement *only* after repeated tries to help a person who was stubborn, arrogant, or bullheaded and who just wouldn't listen to common sense. Invariably, that person would get into some kind of mess and wish they had listened to Annie Ruth, and had acted on her advice. She would let them know that they brought this on themselves, as well as *how* they brought it on themselves.

NOTE: At first glance, this may not sound very compassionate. And it can surely be used to spite someone while enjoying their suffering. But Annie Ruth's compassion always made room for a person who was now ready to listen. Furthermore, the people who received her tough love welcomed it, because they knew that, underneath her firmness, she really *did* care about them and wanted the best for them. But as she would remind them, *I can teach it to you, but I can't learn it for you.*

Annie Ruth's Truth

Don't stop when you FEEL better; stop when it IS better.

MEANING

Annie Ruth is a great nurse. Even now, as I write this book, I am sometimes surprised at the things she comes up with. I am 64, she is 86, and she *still* says things I've never heard, which surprises *her*. We both enjoy a good laugh when this happens.

This statement is a recent example. It came about as I was dealing with a nagging cold. After she found out I had stopped taking medications because I *felt* better, she uttered this Annie Ruth's Truth – straight through the telephone into my consciousness.

I was taken aback, amazed again, but not surprised at her continued genius for wordplay and common-sense wisdom – in the same sentence! I just shook my head and laughed out loud. We laughed together.

Annie Ruth's Truth

I'm broke as the Ten Commandments and happy as a Lark.

MEANING

This is a powerful play on words. It is usually uttered in response to someone who asks *How are you doing, today?* It can be translated to mean *Life is challenging, but I am up to the challenge.*

The statement says it all. It is, in a nutshell, a great response to the vicissitudes of life. It points to the reality that no matter what challenges life sends our way we have power to meet them with the strength of our spirit. To be happy as a Lark (a bird with a beautiful song) while being broke (in more ways than not having money) is a testament to the power of God within us, a power that can sustain us in our difficult times. It speaks of faith, hope, and trust. It speaks to the truth that as tough as life can be, we are blessed nonetheless – blessed to even be alive.

So *sing* like a Lark. Let joy be your song no matter the challenges, for that joy becomes inspiration for others. It becomes hope. It becomes light for those in darkness.

To be broke does not mean we are broken. Though the Ten Commandments, written on stone, were smashed by Moses, they live on. You can be as *broke as the Ten Commandments and happy as a Lark* because you, too, live on. And to be alive is a happiness worth singing about.

Annie Ruth's Truth

Don't put that washing out, 'cause it ain't clean.

MEANING

This refers to putting one's just-washed clothes on the clothes-line. Of course, anyone can see your clothes just hanging there. When it comes to truth-telling, this Annie Ruth's Truth is saying not to put that story out, don't put that lie out there where everybody can see it and hear about it, because it is not the truth and everybody is going to see it for what it is, eventually. So *don't put that washing out, 'cause it ain't clean.*

The underlying proverb is that it is better
to tell the truth than get caught in a lie.

108

Annie Ruth's Truth

You're pickin' in high cotton and you'll soon get your 100!

MEANING

This is a warning. It means you're getting in over your head, or you're biting off more than you can chew. If you pick 100 pounds of cotton, you have to carry it, too. It is heavy and nobody is going to carry it for you. So if you keep doing what you're doing, you're going to have a burden on your hands you don't want. It's going to be all on you; there will be no one but yourself to blame and there will be no one to save you from yourself. So you better think about what you're doing before you get yourself in real trouble, deeper than you can handle, 'cause *you're pickin' in high cotton and you'll soon get your 100!*

109

Annie Ruth's Truth

Love is blind but the neighbours ain't.

MEANING

You better act like you have some sense. If you're going to do what you're doing, you better know where you're doing it, 'cause *every shut eye ain't sleep and every goodbye ain't gone* (#94), and the way you two are carrying on wherever and whenever, you're getting lost in it all and losing your heads. Just because you're in love doesn't mean you can do what you want anytime you want, or anywhere you want. You need to think about how you look to other people, 'cause *love is blind, but the neighbours ain't*. Stop acting like you don't have any home training. I'm trying to help you out before you get found out. And *I can teach it to you, but I can't learn it for you.*

*Annie Ruth, 84, in conversation with a friend on the phone
talking about the weather:*

I am tired of all this bad weather we've been having. It's been keeping me cooped up, keeping me from going outside.

FRIEND: Well, I hear the sun's actually gonna be coming out for a minute today.

ANNIE RUTH: Well then, I'll be outside – **for a *minute!***

*Annie Ruth, 84, says to me as we are talking about
the problems she is having with a bad knee,*

I won the Miss Poise contest in my school when I was a young woman. I use to keep my back straight, head up and just go. My brother, Elvester, use to make fun of me. He told me one day, *Girl, you hold your head up so much if there was money on the ground you'd walk right over it.*

Well now, especially with a bad knee, I tend to keep my head down so I can see where I'm going and know where I'm turning! *(She says this with a lot of attitude.)*

Oh, I'm very intent on knowing where my feet are now, so I don't trip.

Annie Ruth's Truth

**Yeah, I use to look up and just go.
Now I look down to see
where I'm going.**

Kind of ironic.

EPILOGUE

NNIE RUTH'S
truths represent a form of folk wisdom and wit that is fading
from American culture, as its carriers leave us. This wisdom is
timeless in that it incorporates humour and common sense that
speak to the common challenges and realities of being human.
As we now live in a world where media and technology domi-
nate the way in which we take in knowledge, information, and
entertainment, this less-modern style of humour and mode of
giving and receiving wisdom can get overlooked, if not lost, in
the shuffle of countless experts and pundits vying for our eyes
and ears on television. Likewise, there is no end to magazines
that call for our attention in grocery lines as they shout titillat-
ing word bites at us.

Annie Ruth's truths remind us of the genius of everyday,
salt-of-the-earth people. Wisdom is available to all who seek it.
And humour is the healing balm that can make tough love pal-
atable. This is the lasting value of Annie Ruth's truths. The sayings may harken to times past, but they have also been time tested.
Rooted in the rural agricultural landscape of the American Deep
South, I believe this organic art form of wordplay and wisdom
will become a treasure of American culture in the years ahead. It
already is for many.

DAVID PRESTON SHARP

is a writer, performer, poet, musician, and educator. A Presbyterian minister, he has served churches in Los Angeles, San Francisco, Oakland, and Richmond, California. He was a founding faculty member of the Fox Institute for Creation Spirituality, in Boulder, Colorado. He has performed on Broadway and in Hollywood movies and television shows. David holds a BFA in drama from the University of Southern California, an MDiv from San Francisco Theological Seminary, an MSpEd from Santa Clara University, and a DMin from the University of Creation Spirituality. In September 2020, David and his wife, Dr. Jeannine Goode-Allen, launched the Good&Sharp Studios, a home for spirituality and the arts in Boulder, and will host their first retreat in 2021 for spiritual creatives.

ANNIE RUTH SHARP

is the mother of David, Vanessa, and Celanese. She is a grand-mother to nine and great-grandmother to seven. In addition to being a homemaker, she has also worked as a healthcare and teach-er's assistant, retail clerk, and housemother at a Christian private boarding school. She is a beloved member of Westhills Presby-terian Church in Atlanta, Georgia, where her late husband, Rev. John Sharp, was the pastor. She continues to enjoy family, friends, and strangers alike, and to receive deep fulfillment from helping people live a better life.

WOOD LAKE

**IMAGINING, LIVING, AND TELLING
THE FAITH STORY.**

WOOD LAKE IS THE FAITH STORY COMPANY.

It has told
- the story of the seasons of the earth, the people of God, and the place and purpose of faith in the world;
- the story of the faith journey, from birth to death;
- the story of Jesus and the churches that carry his message.

Wood Lake has been telling stories for more than 35 years. During that time, it has given form and substance to the words, songs, pictures, and ideas of hundreds of storytellers.

Those stories have taken a multitude of forms – parables, poems, drawings, prayers, epiphanies, songs, books, paintings, hymns, curricula – all driven by a common mission of serving those on the faith journey.

WOOD LAKE PUBLISHING INC.
485 Beaver Lake Road
Kelowna, BC, Canada V4V 1S5
250.766.2778

www.woodlake.com